Drawing
Cats

Illustrated by Katy Bratun

ISBN 0-448-42595-5   A B C D E F G H I J

HAVE FUN DRAWING CATS!

Helpful Hints

🐾 Work slowly, one step at a time.

🐾 Use a sharp pencil with an eraser.

🐾 Look carefully at the instructional drawing to see:
    the sizes of the shapes in relation to one another,
    the lengths of the lines,
    the sizes of the curves,
    the sizes of the angles, and
    where lines cross other lines.

🐾 Draw lightly at first. This is called sketching.

🐾 For a finished look, darken the important lines and erase the lines that are unimportant, such as the circles and rectangles.

🐾 Remember, the more you draw, the better you get, so draw a lot!

🐾 Just as your handwriting is unique, so is your drawing style.

FACE FROM FRONT

 1 First draw a circle for the head. Draw two straight lines through the center of the circle. Then add two triangle shapes for the ears.

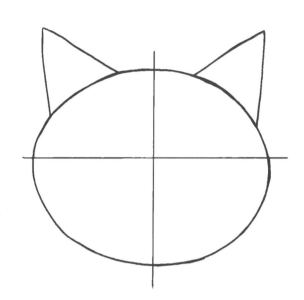

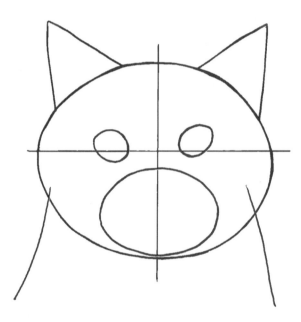

 2 Draw two more circles for the eyes. Then draw another circle for the muzzle. Add two curved lines for the neck.

 3 Fill in the nose and mouth shapes. Give the ears a little more detail by adding two lines. Add curved lines to the neck.

Now outline the shape
with curved lines.

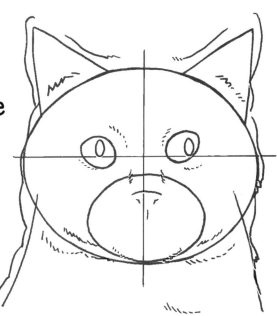

 Erase the extra lines.
Fill in the whiskers and fur lines.

HEAD AT AN ANGLE

 1 Begin with a circle for the head. Draw two lines through the circle, slightly to the right. Then add two triangle shapes for the ears.

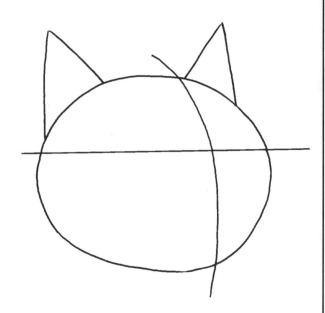

 2 Draw in two circles for the eyes. Add a larger circle for the muzzle. Then draw two curved lines for the neck.

 **3** Give your cat a nose and mouth. Sketch some curved lines in the neck and face. Add curved lines to the ears.

4 Smooth out the edges and continue to sketch in more detailed lines.

5 Erase the geometric shapes and finish smoothing out the edges. Darken the lines around the eyes. Add whiskers, and finish it off by filling in fur lines.

SIDE VIEW OF BODY

1

Draw shapes to begin the head and body of your cat. Connect the head and body shapes with two curved lines for the neck.

2

Draw smaller circles for the legs and paws. Connect the circles with curved lines for the legs. Add a circle for the ear.

3

Draw an oval for the tail. Add two oval shapes in the head for the muzzle. Smooth out the lines for the body.

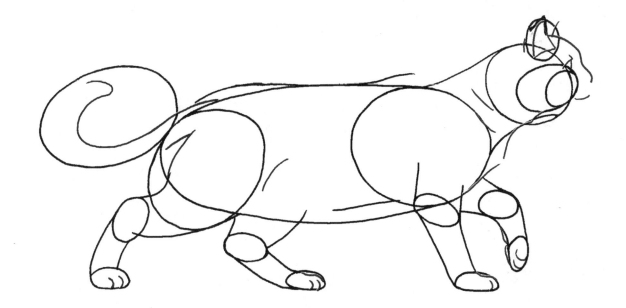

 Add more details by giving your cat a tail, eye, and ear. Sketch in some lines on the paws. Outline the head and neck with curved lines.

Erase the extra lines. Fill in your cat with fur lines.

FRONT VIEW OF BODY

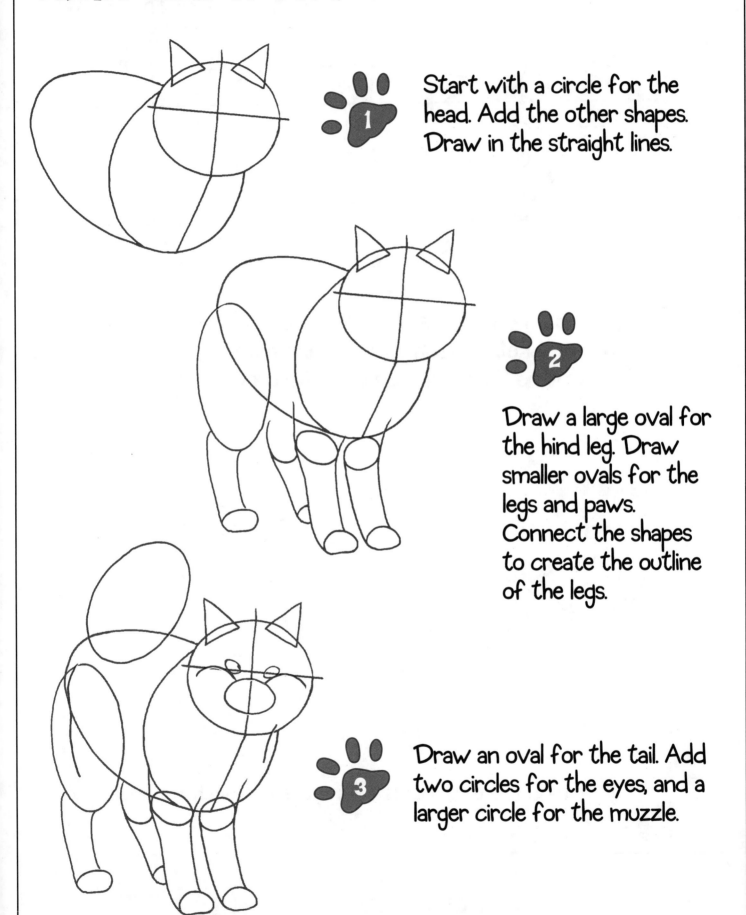

1 Start with a circle for the head. Add the other shapes. Draw in the straight lines.

2 Draw a large oval for the hind leg. Draw smaller ovals for the legs and paws. Connect the shapes to create the outline of the legs.

3 Draw an oval for the tail. Add two circles for the eyes, and a larger circle for the muzzle.

4

Give some detail to the paws. Draw in the tail. Sketch in curved lines to smooth out the body, head, and ears of your cat.

5

Smooth out the edges, erase the extra lines, and add the remaining details.

ARCHED BACK

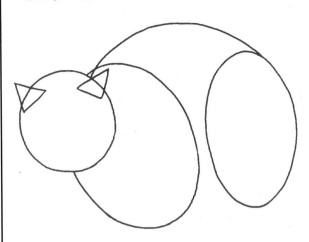

Begin with a circle for the head, and two triangles for the ears. Draw the shapes for the body, and connect them with a curved line. Make a straight line on the bottom.

Draw shapes for the legs and paws. Draw curved lines connecting the shapes for the legs. Draw a straight line through the head.

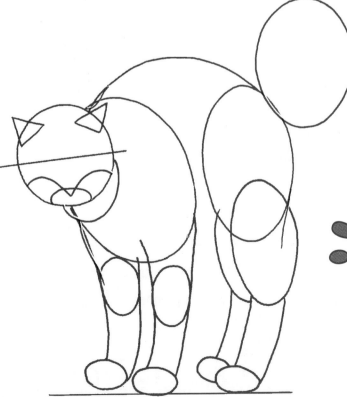

Add an oval for the tail. Add curved lines in the face and neck. Smooth out some of the edges.

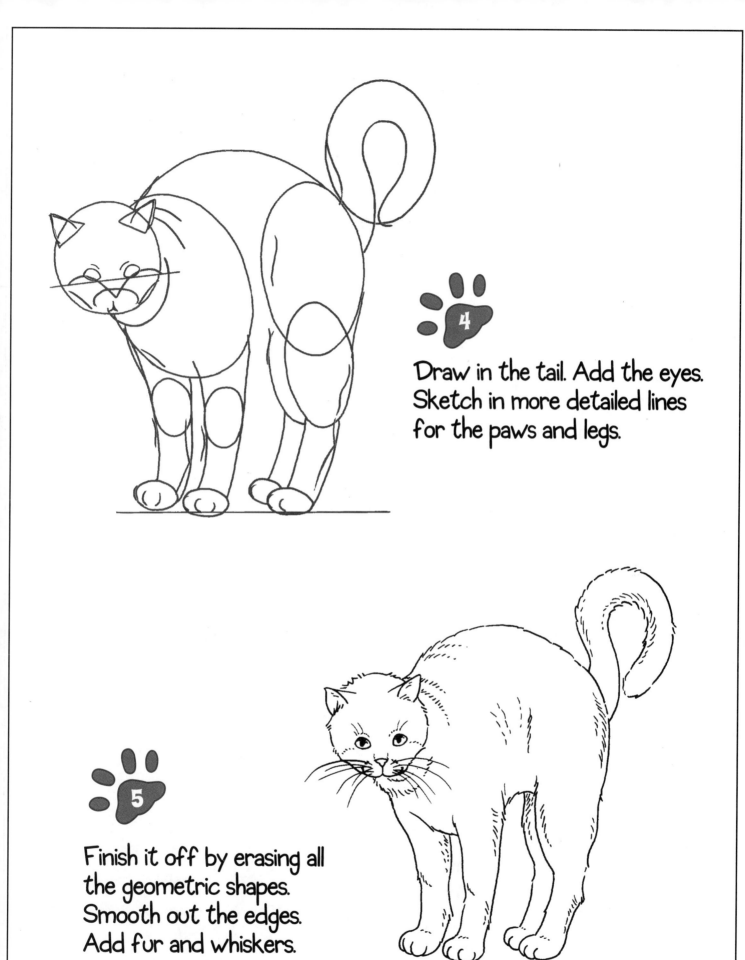

4

Draw in the tail. Add the eyes. Sketch in more detailed lines for the paws and legs.

5

Finish it off by erasing all the geometric shapes. Smooth out the edges. Add fur and whiskers.

SITTING

 Draw shapes for the head, neck, and body of the cat. Add triangle shapes for the ears. Draw additional lines.

 Add more oval shapes for the legs and paws. Connect the ovals to create the legs. Fill in curved lines for the muzzle.

 Give your cat eyes and a mouth. Draw an oval for the tail. Round out some of the edges.

Add detailed lines to the ears, neck, and paws. Fill in the tail.

Erase all of the extra lines. Add the finishing touches.

CLEANING PAW

1 Start with the head and body shapes. Put in the curved lines to begin the outline of the body. Add a straight line at the bottom.

2 Add three smaller ovals for the front legs and paws. Connect the shapes to form the legs. Draw a larger oval for the tail.

3 Add shapes to create the hind legs. Fill in the curved lines for the muzzle. Add a circle for the front ear. Add a small triangle for the back ear.

4

Draw in the tail. Add some curved lines to the paws. Sketch in the front ear. Smooth out the shape of the head. Add the eye and tongue.

5

"Clean up" this cat by erasing the extra lines and filling in the remaining details.

LYING DOWN

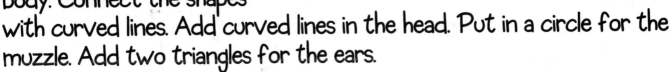

Begin by drawing a circle for the head. Add the other shapes for the body. Connect the shapes with curved lines. Add curved lines in the head. Put in a circle for the muzzle. Add two triangles for the ears.

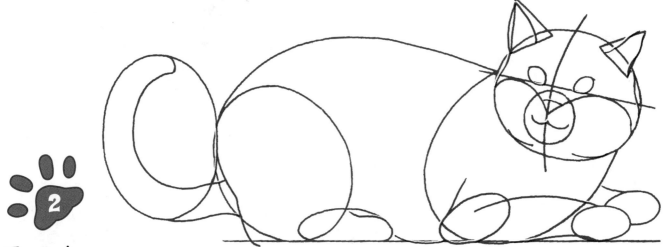

First draw an oval for the tail. Then outline the shape of the tail. Add ovals for the front legs and paws. Give your cat a mouth, nose, and eyes. Smooth out the ears.

Round out the edges. Erase the extra lines. Add whiskers and fur lines.

SLEEPING

1

Draw a large circle for the body. Add a smaller circle for the head. Connect the shapes with a curved line on the top. Draw curved lines on the head. Put in a circle for the muzzle. Add two triangles for the ears.

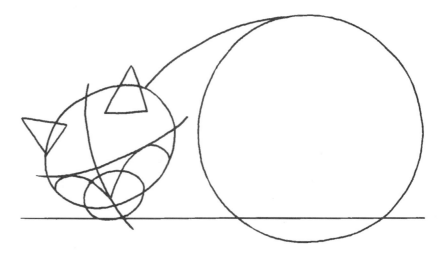

2

Draw an oval for the tail. Then outline the shape of the tail. Add shapes for the paws. Put in a nose, mouth, and two curved lines for the eyes. Smooth out the ears and shape of the head.

3

Erase the extra lines, and make your cat furry.

KITTEN-SIDE VIEW

1 First, draw a circle for the head. Next, draw two ovals for the body. Connect the shapes with lines. Add two triangles for the ears.

2 Draw smaller circles for the legs and paws. Connect the circles with curved lines for the legs. Draw another circle for the ball. Add a straight line for your kitten to stand on.

3 Next, draw an oval for the tail. Add a straight line to the left ear, and a curved line to the right ear. Draw a line through the head. Add a circle for the muzzle, and curved lines below the straight line.

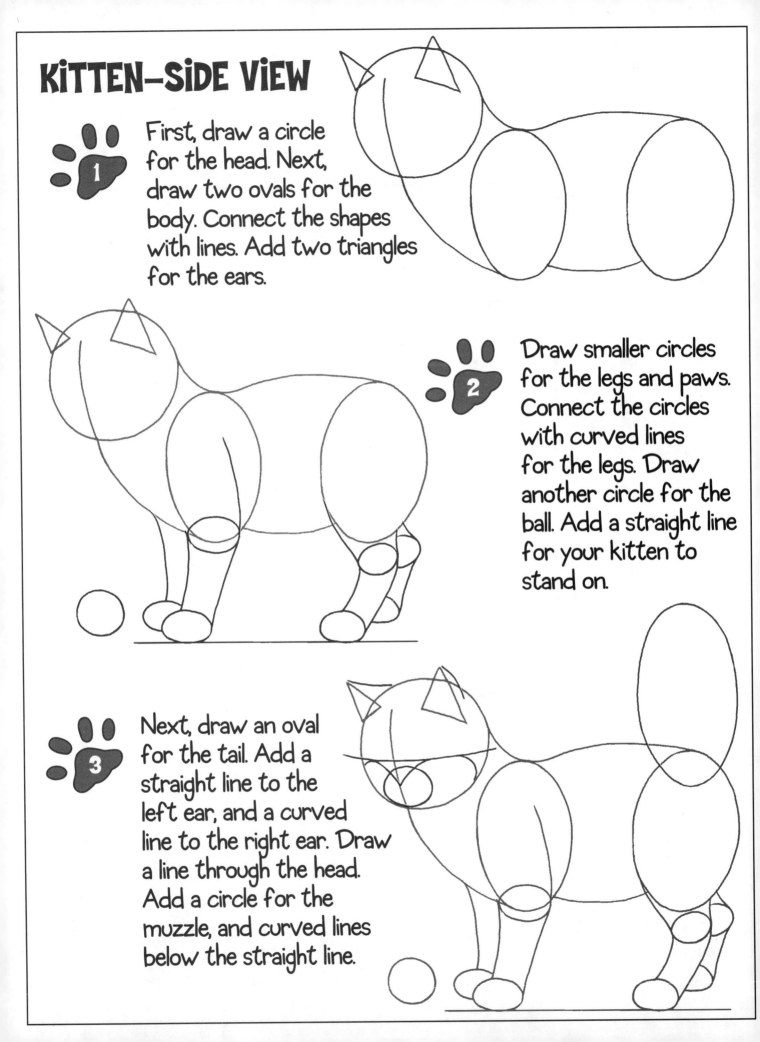

4

Draw in the tail. Give your kitten's paws some detailed lines. Draw curved lines for the neck. Add the eyes, nose, and mouth. Sketch in some fur lines. Give the ball some polka dots.

5

Finish it off by erasing the geometric lines, smoothing out the edges, and adding the last touches, like more fur lines and whiskers.

KiTTEN—FRONT VIEW

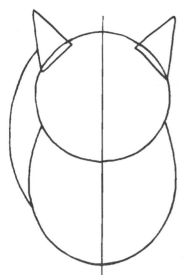

 Start with a circle for the head. Add two triangles for the ears. Draw the other shape for the body. Place a straight line through the center of the shapes. Add a curved line from the body to the ear.

 Draw small ovals for the legs and paws. Connect the shapes to create the legs. Draw two straight lines underneath the paws.

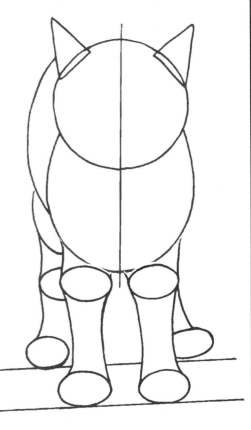

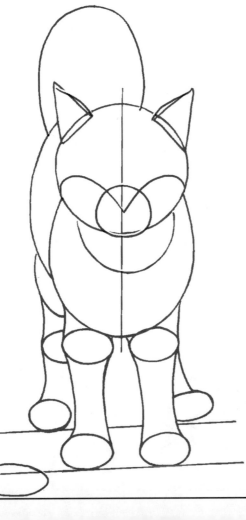

 Draw a curved line for the tail. Add a circle on the head for the muzzle, and the other curved lines. Smooth out the ears. Place a circle and two ovals beside the cat for the ball of yarn.

Add the eyes, nose and mouth. Sketch lines in the face to give the head more detail. Place curved lines in the paws, and on the ball of yarn. Connect the ovals with curved lines for the string. Draw in the tail.

Erase the extra lines. Give your kitten fur and whiskers. Polish off the ball of yarn.

KITTEN-PLAYING

 1 Begin with a circle for the head. Add two triangles for the ears. Draw two more shapes for the body. Then draw a curved line through the three shapes.

 2 Draw two large ovals for the hind legs. Add a curved line through the head. Place a circle for the muzzle. Round out the ears. Add two lines for the neck. Draw a straight line at the bottom.

 3 Start with drawing smaller ovals for your kitten's front legs and paws. Connect the shapes to form the legs. Draw two more circles for the body of the mouse. Add the eyes and nose. Add a curved line for the tail.

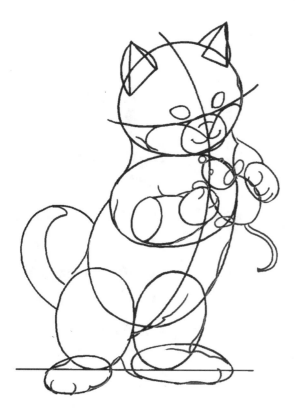

 4

Draw in the tail. Sketch in some detailed lines in the paws and body. Add eyes, ears, a nose and a tail to the mouse.

 5

Polish it off by erasing the geometric shapes and smoothing out the edges. Add fur lines and whiskers.

MOTHER CAT AND KITTEN

Start with the mother cat. Draw shapes for the body and head. Fill in the curved lines. Add the triangle shapes for the ears.

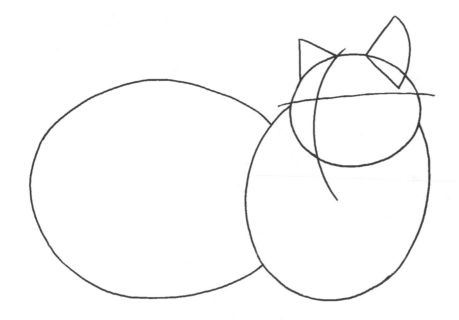

Draw the shapes for the legs and paws. Use curved lines to outline the shapes of the legs. Add a circle for the muzzle. And add curved lines to the face and neck.

3

Place a large oval over the body for the tail. Next add the shapes for the head and body of the kitten.

4

Give your kitten its front legs and paws. Sketch in its muzzle. Draw the mother cat's tail.

5

Start detailing the mother cat. Add nose, mouth, and eyes. Smooth out the ears and legs.

6

Now give more detail to the kitten. Add curved lines to the ears. Fill in the eyes, nose and round out the shape of the body.

Continue sketching in more curved lines.

Erase all of the extra lines. Touch up with final details, like adding fur, whiskers, and darkening the eyes.

COAT PATTERNS—FACE

Tabby

Calico

Bicolor—White and
Solid Color

Color Pointed

SOME COAT PATTERNS—BODY

Coat Patterns on Tabby Varieties

Classic Tabby

Spotted Tabby

Mackerel Tabby

Bicolor—White and solid color

Color Pointed

Calico—White with black and red

NOW DRAW A CAT LIKE THIS ONE ON YOUR OWN!

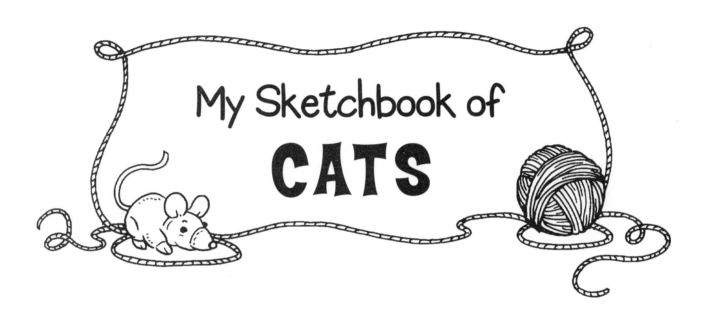

My Sketchbook of
CATS

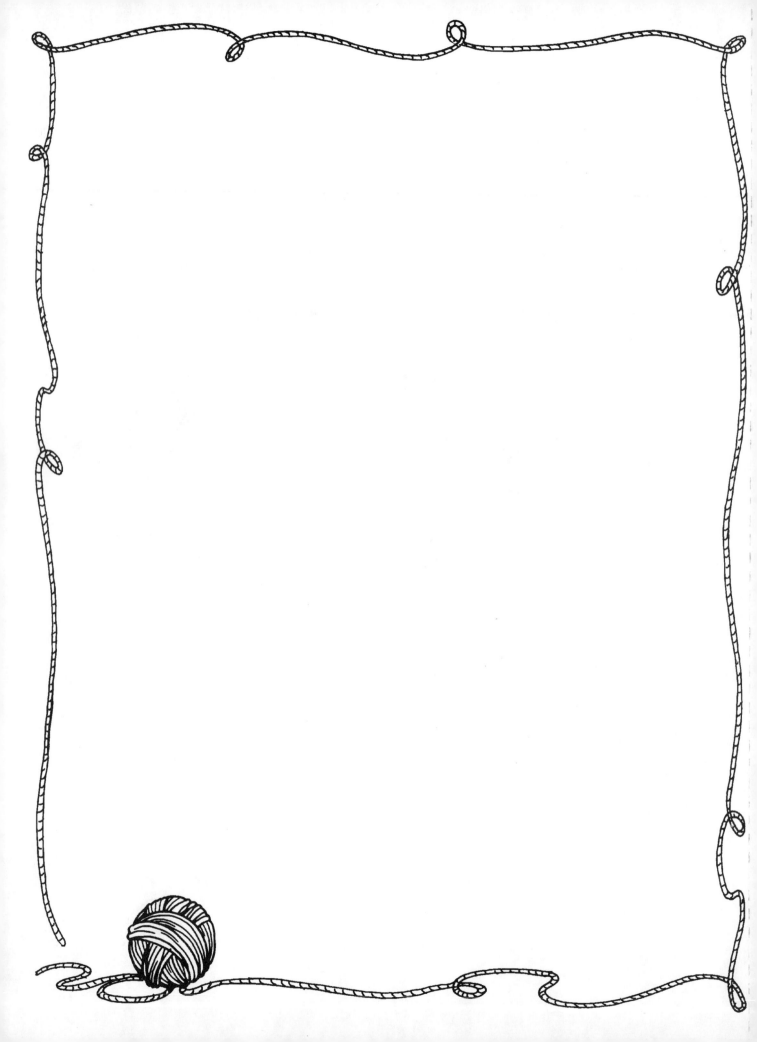

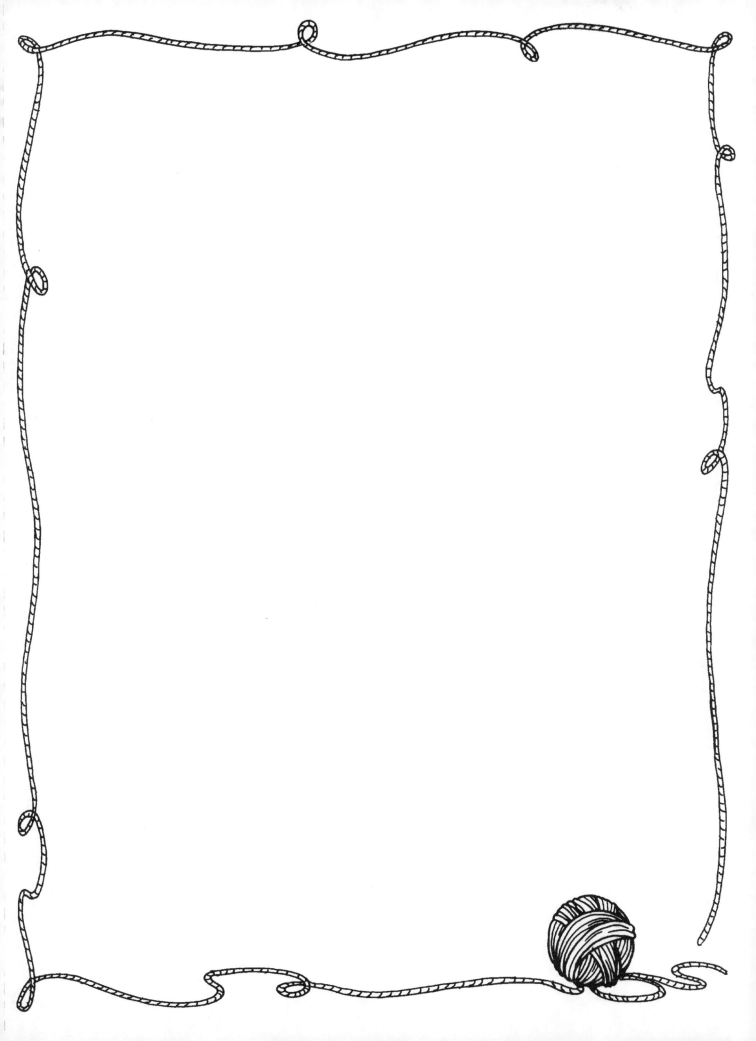

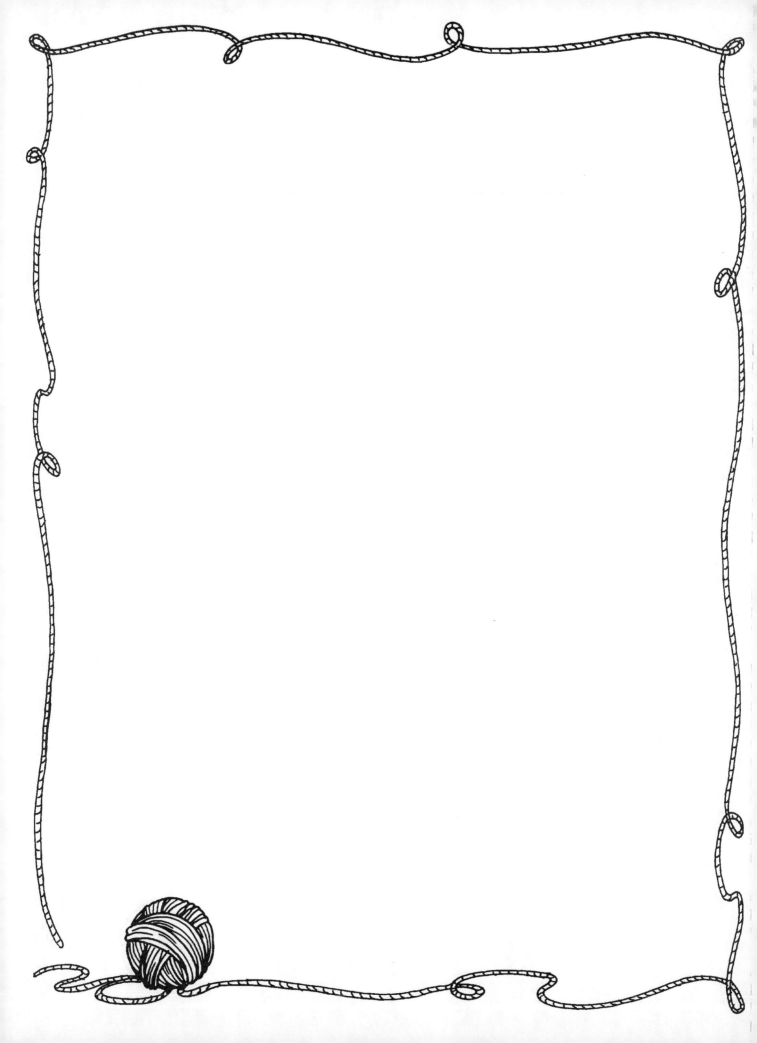

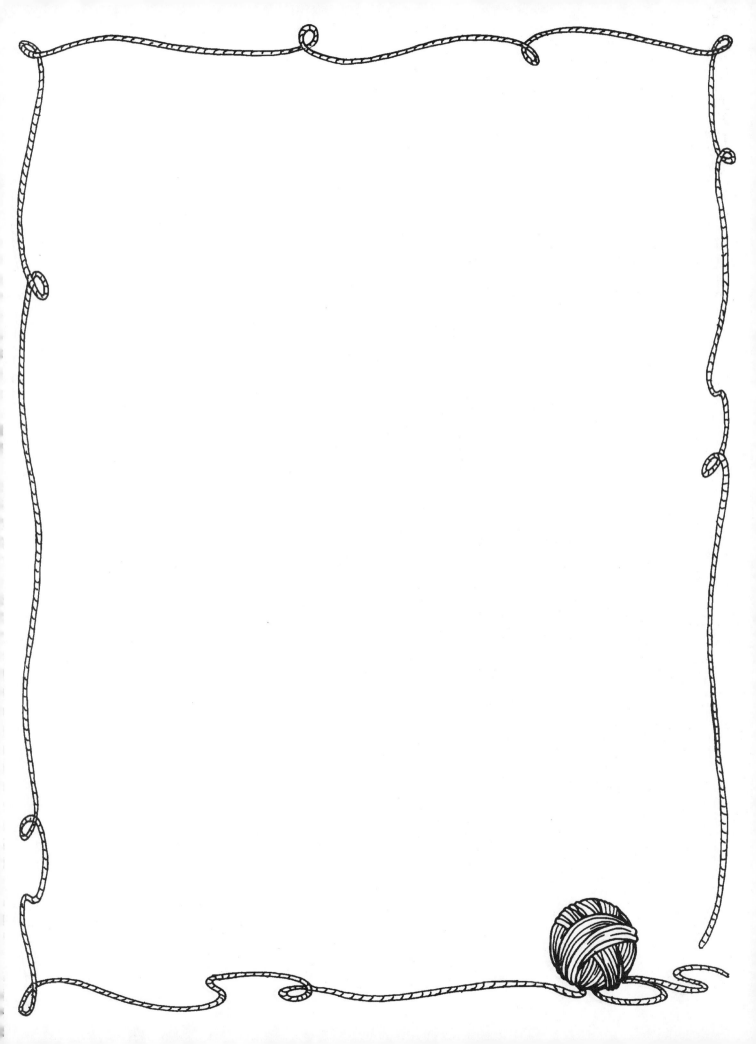

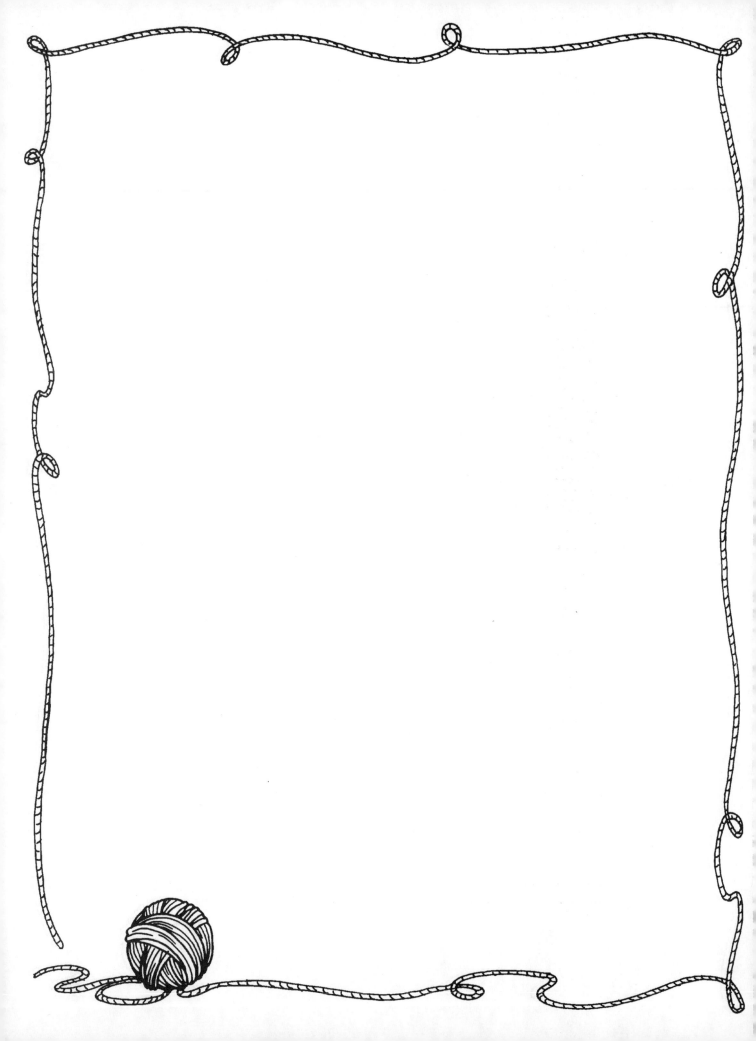

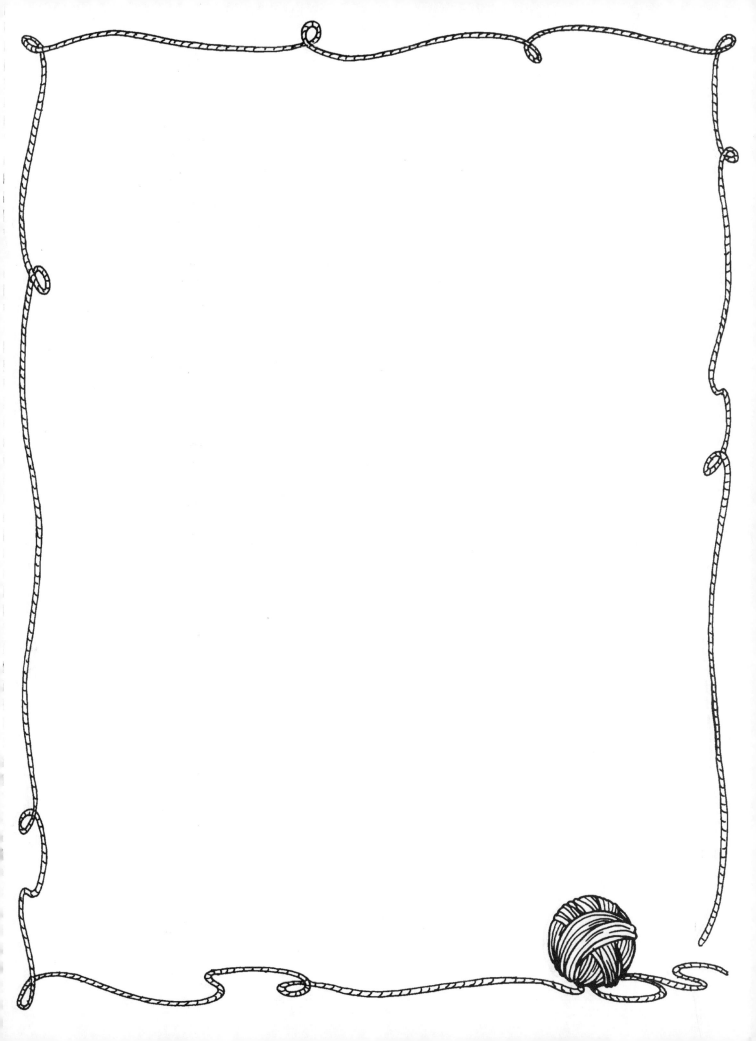

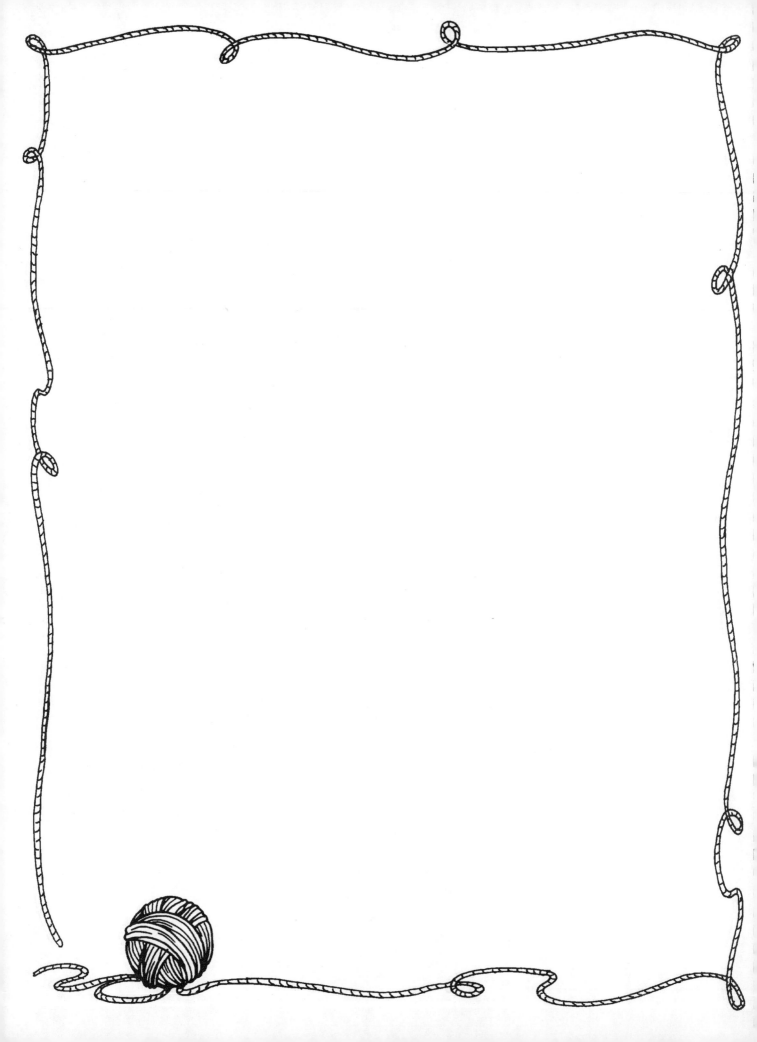

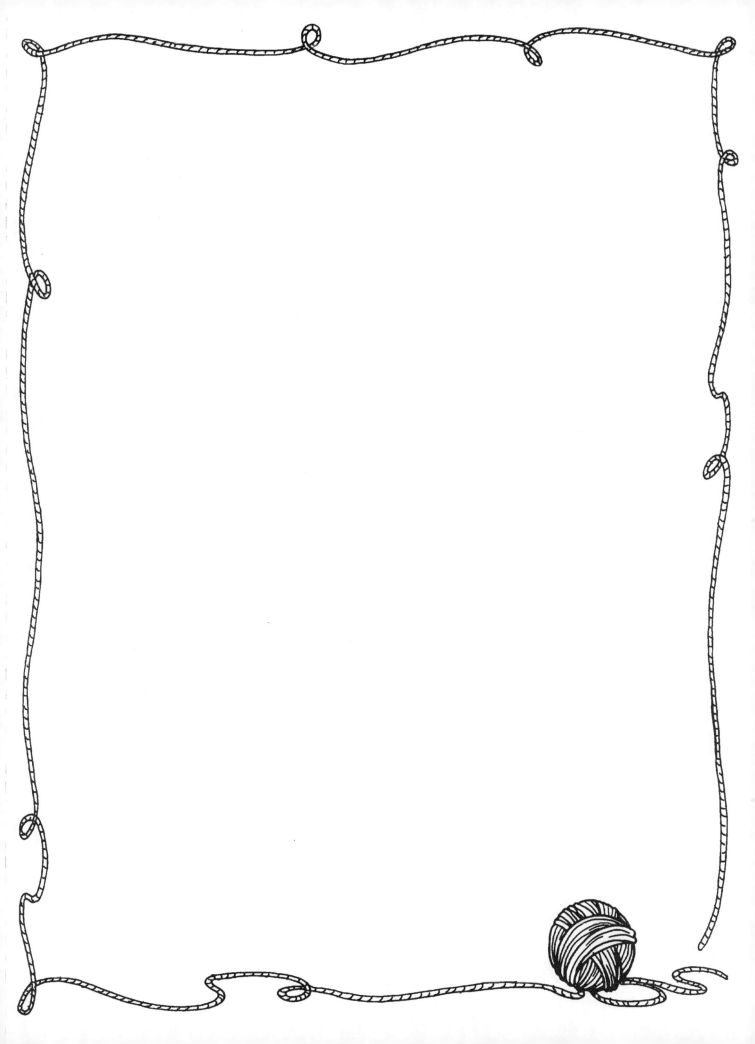

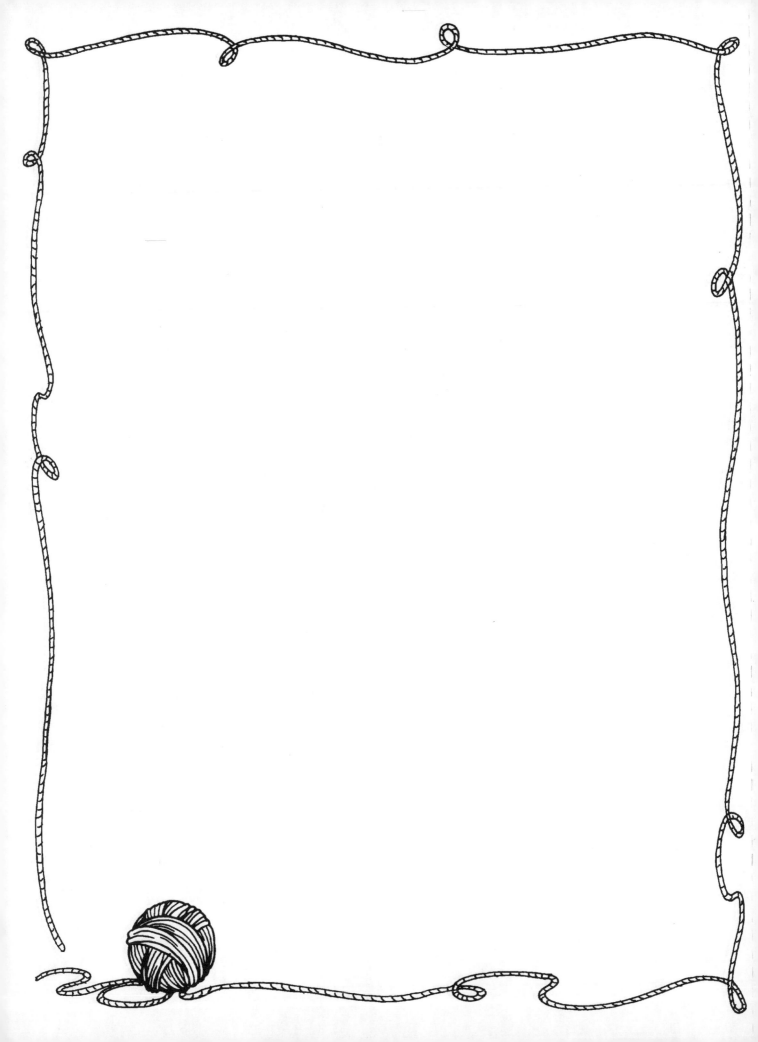

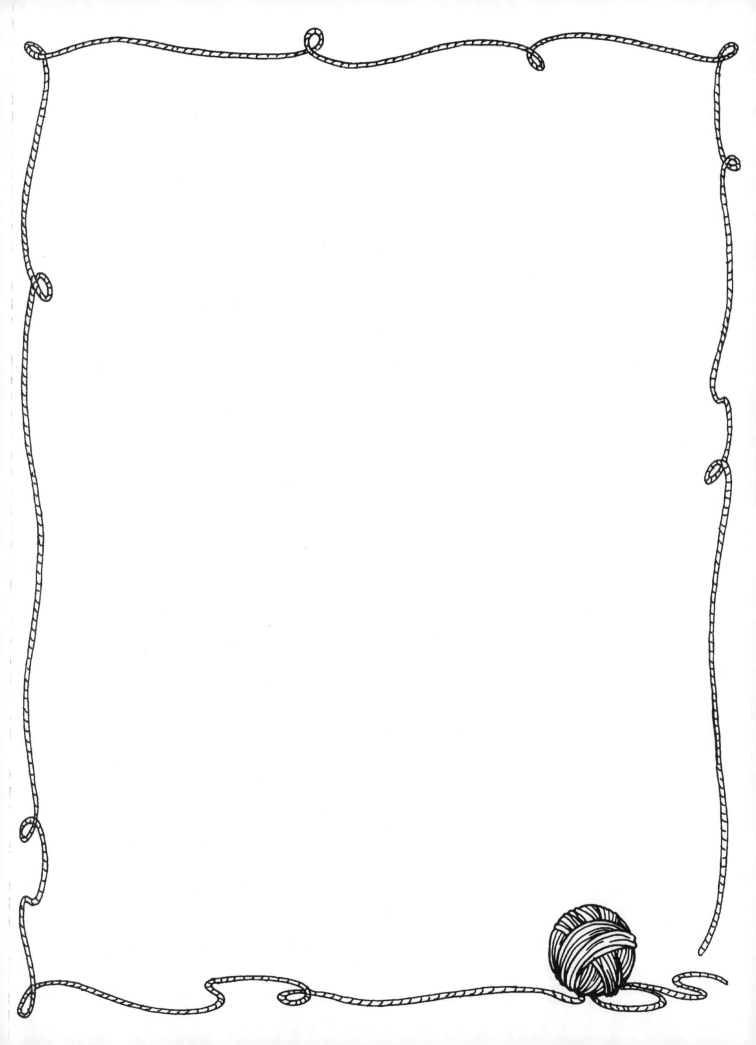

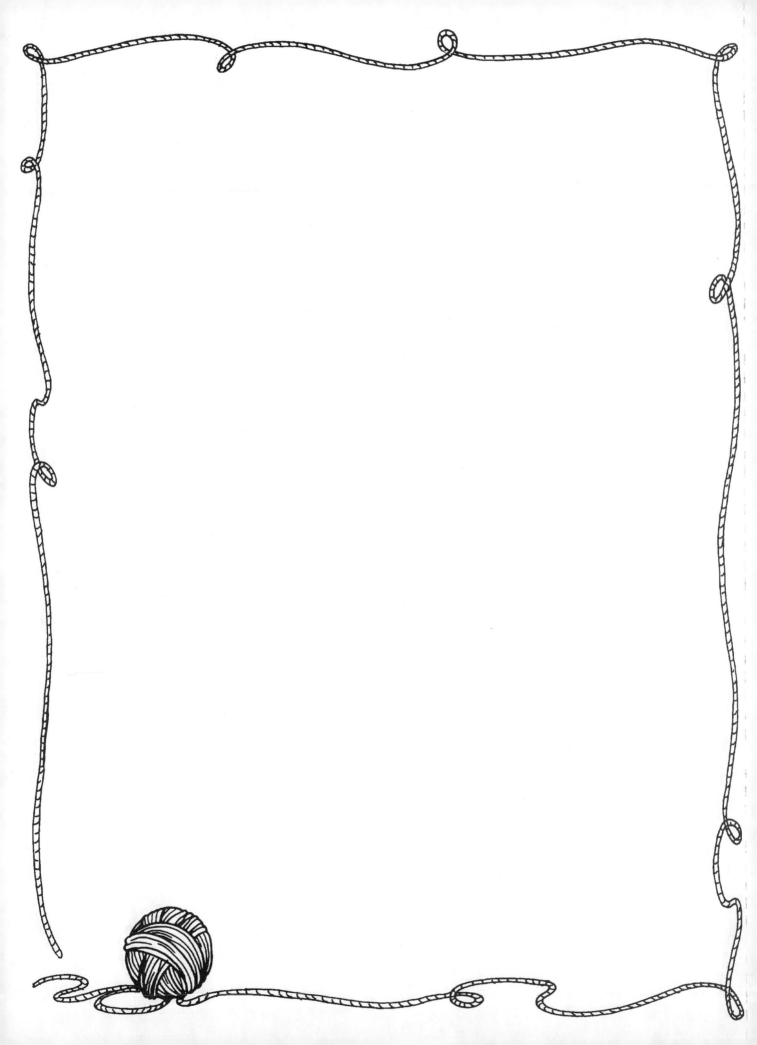

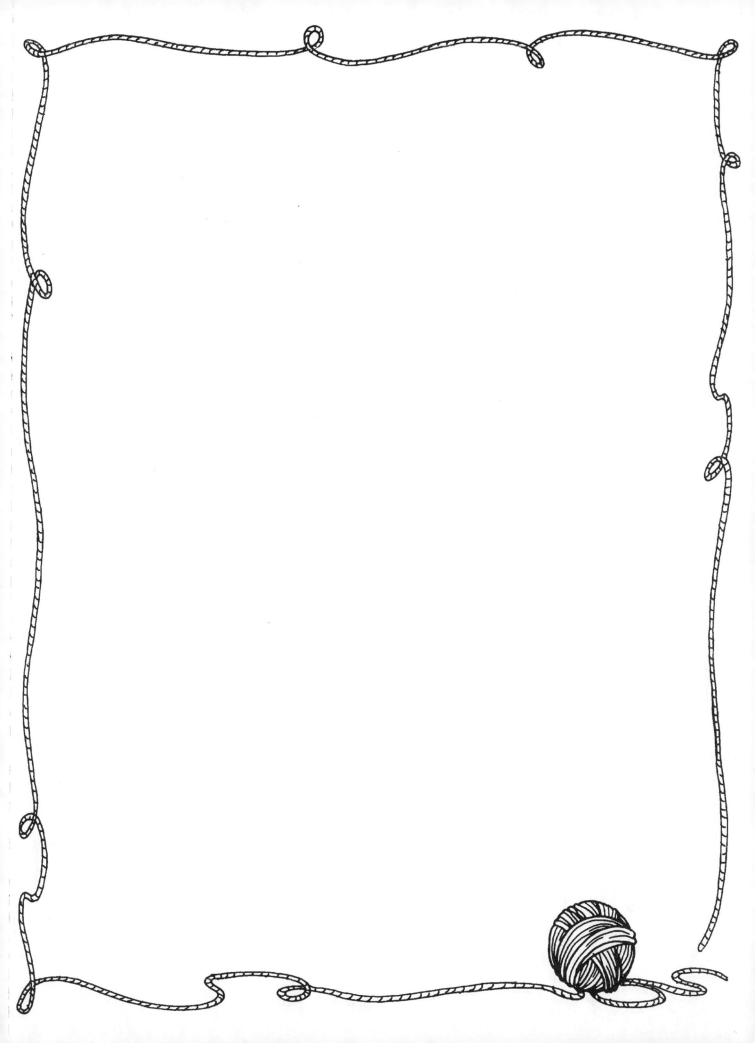

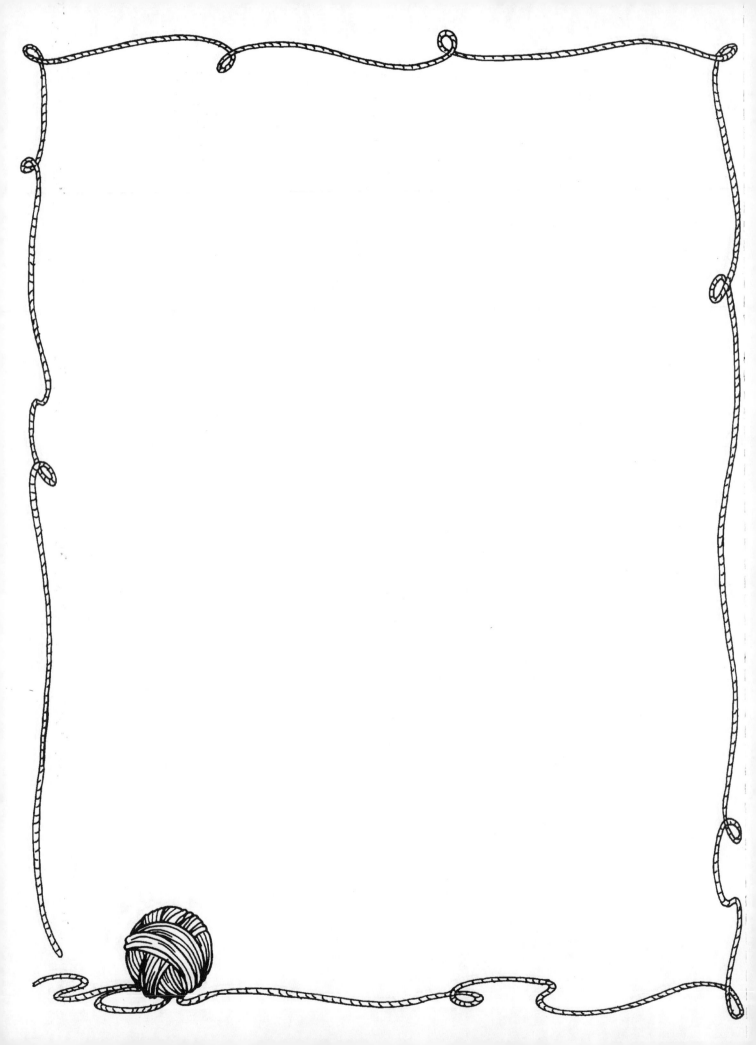

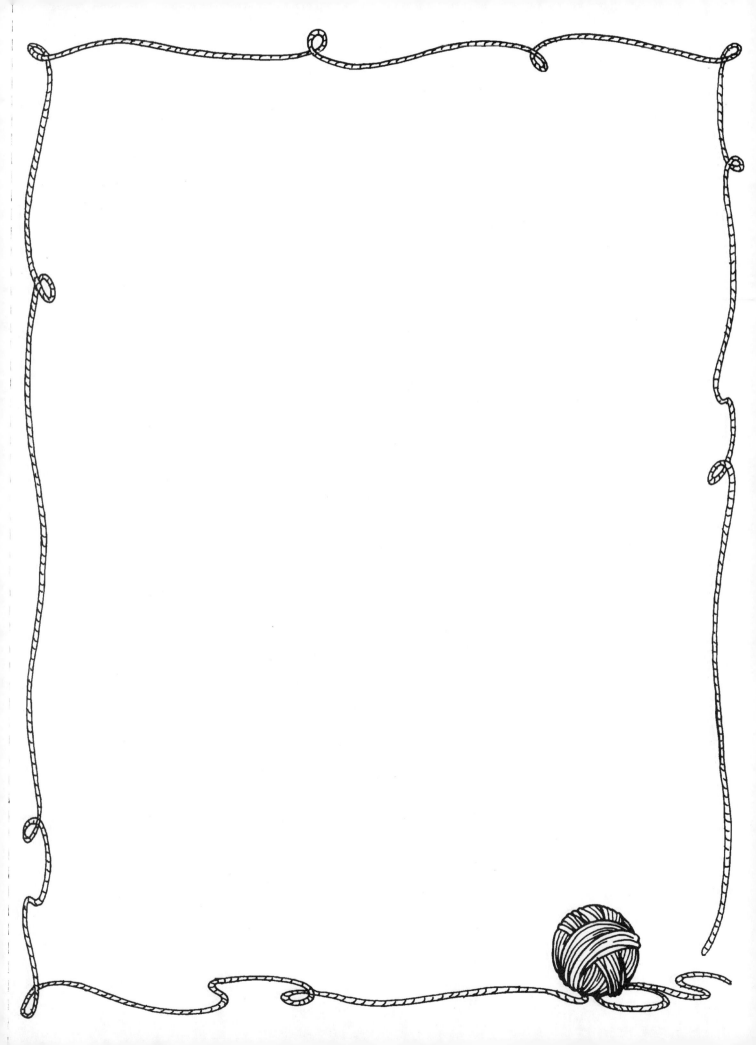

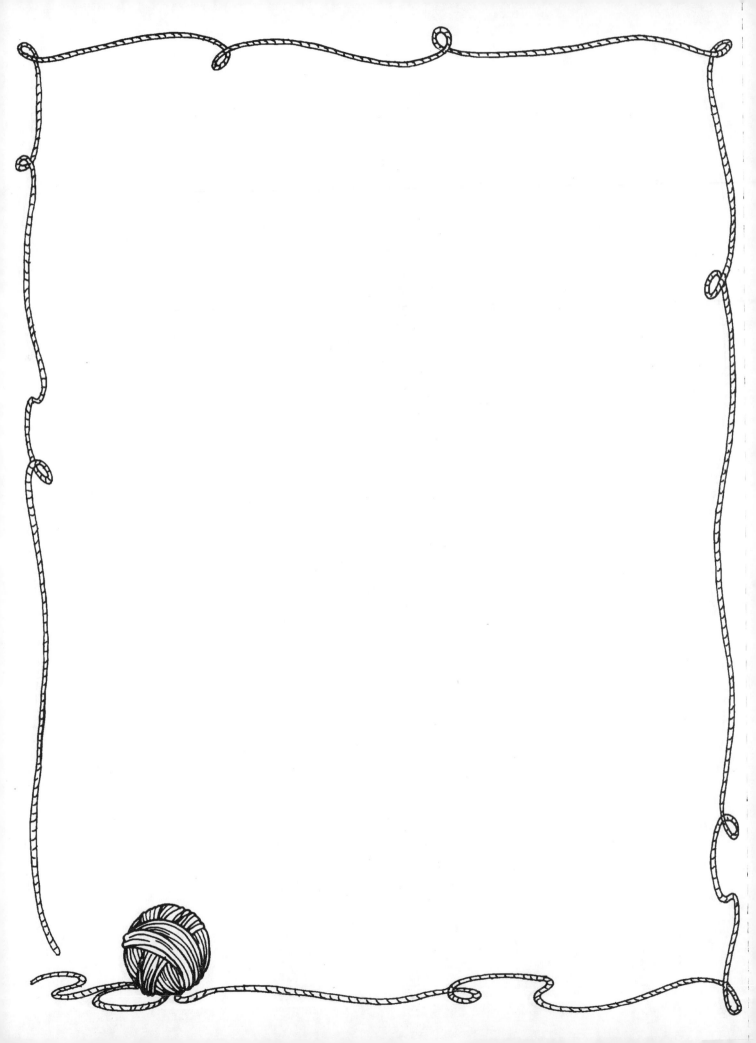

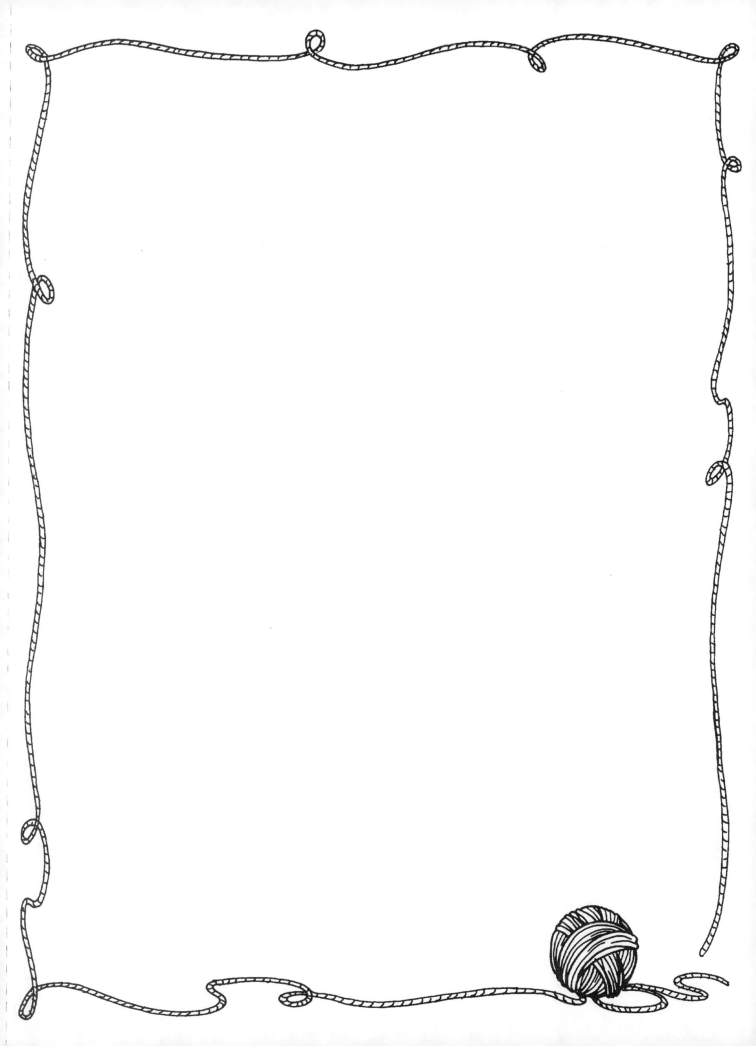

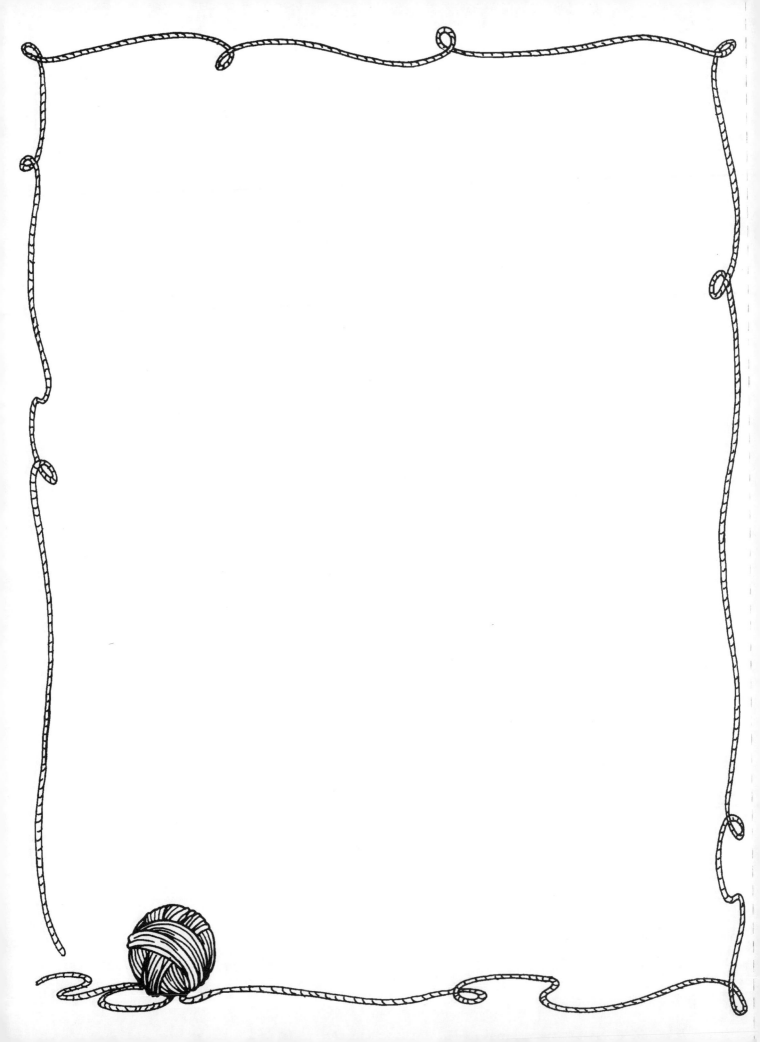

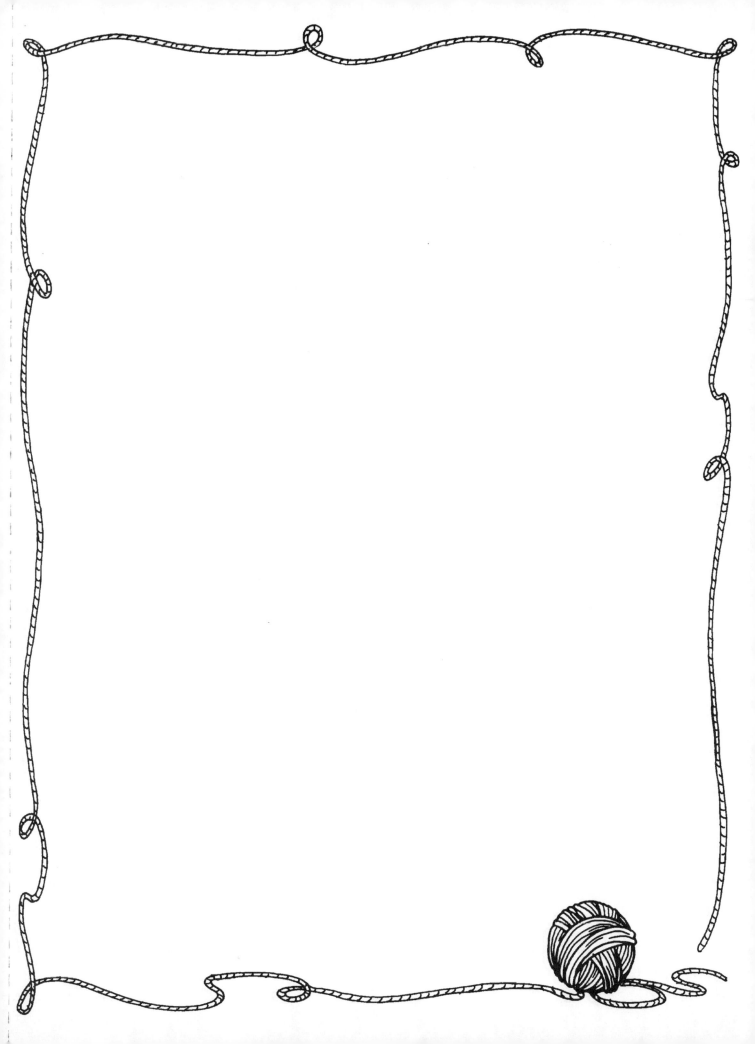

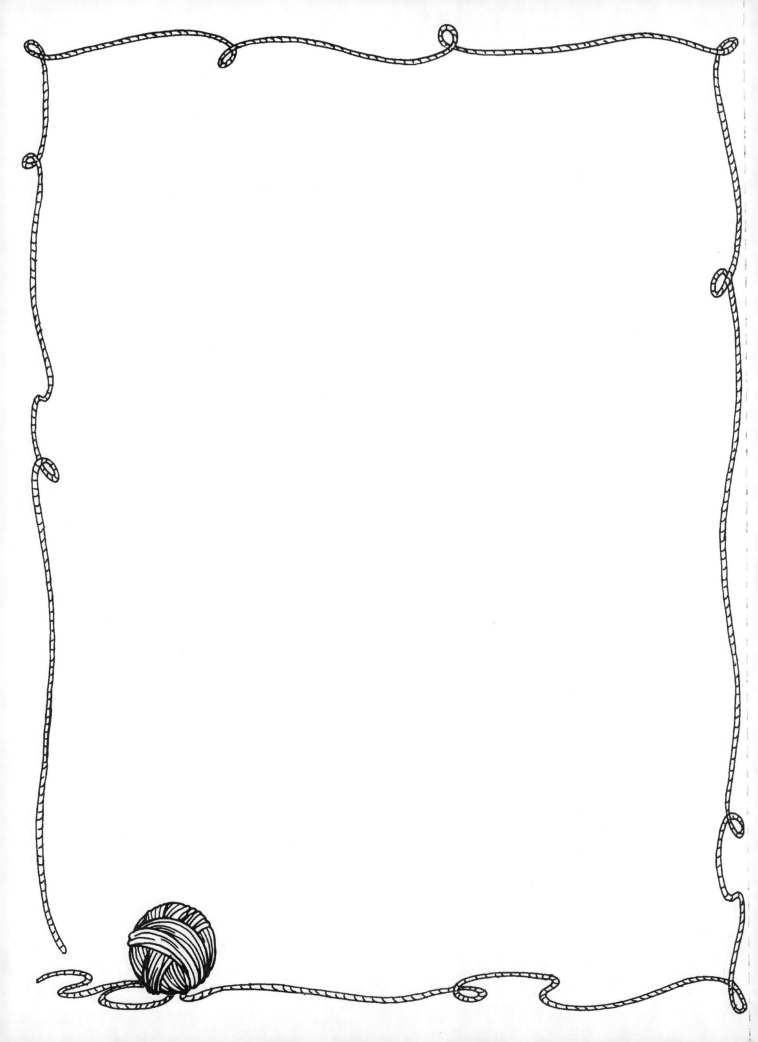

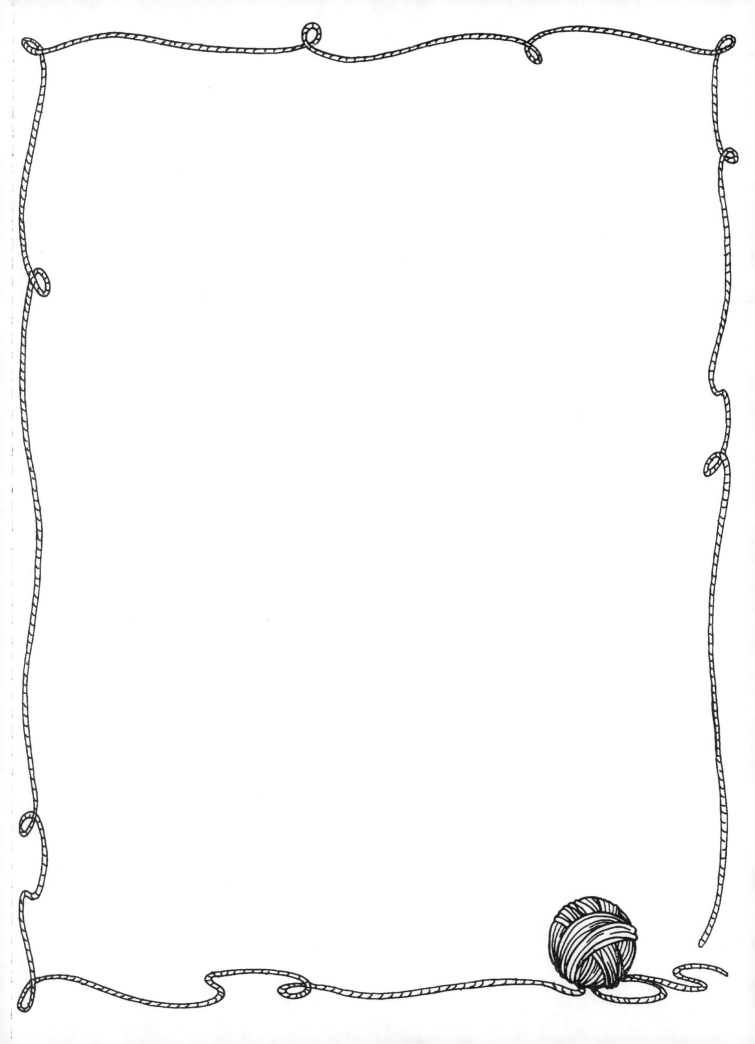

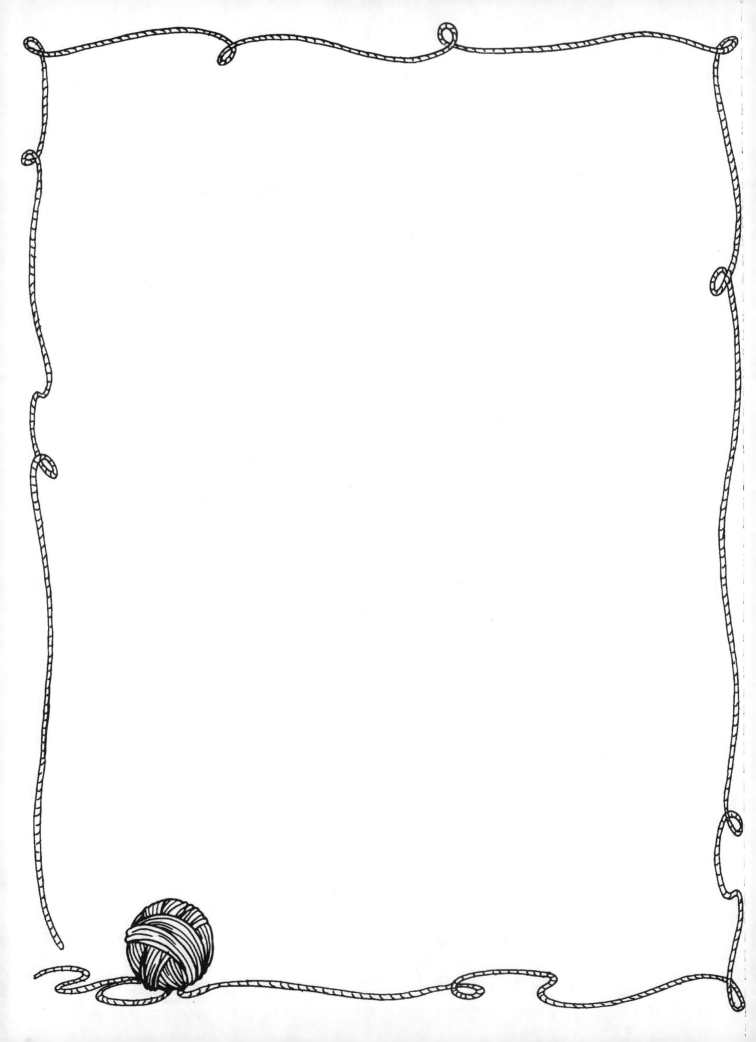

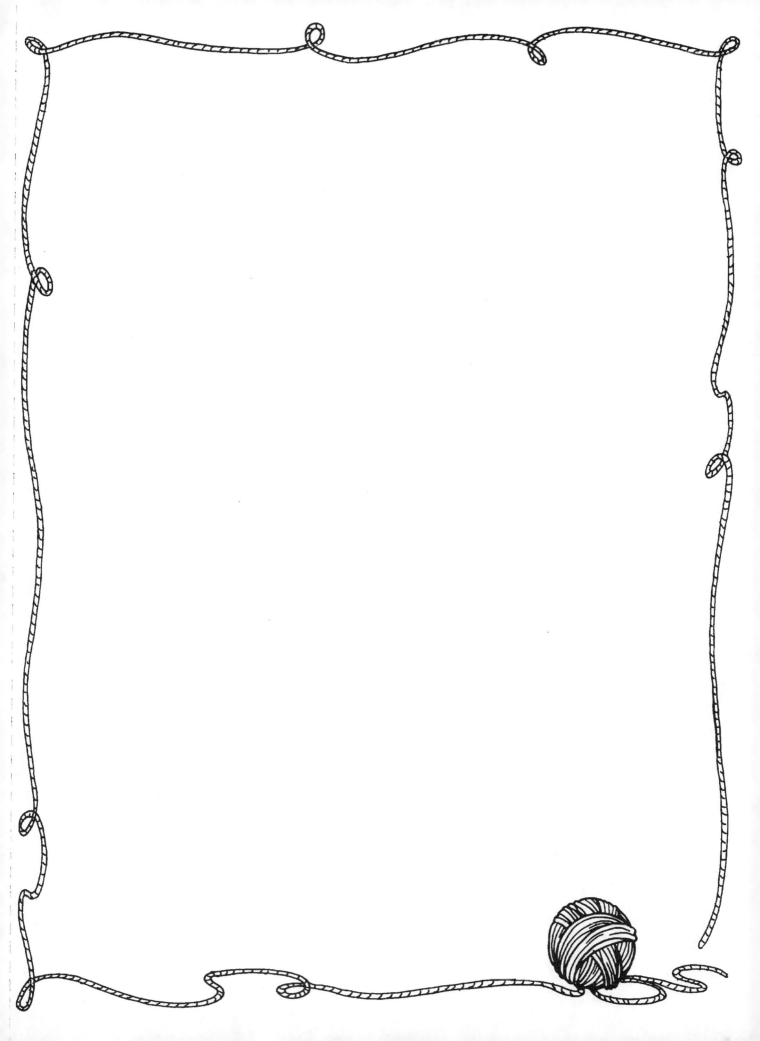

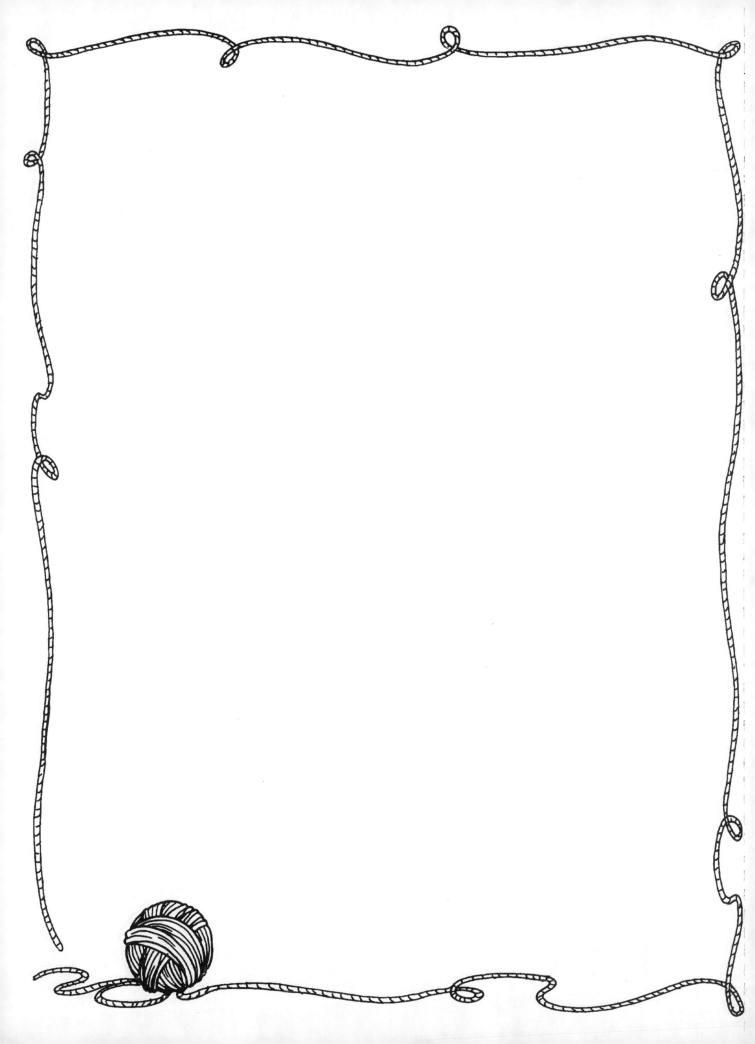

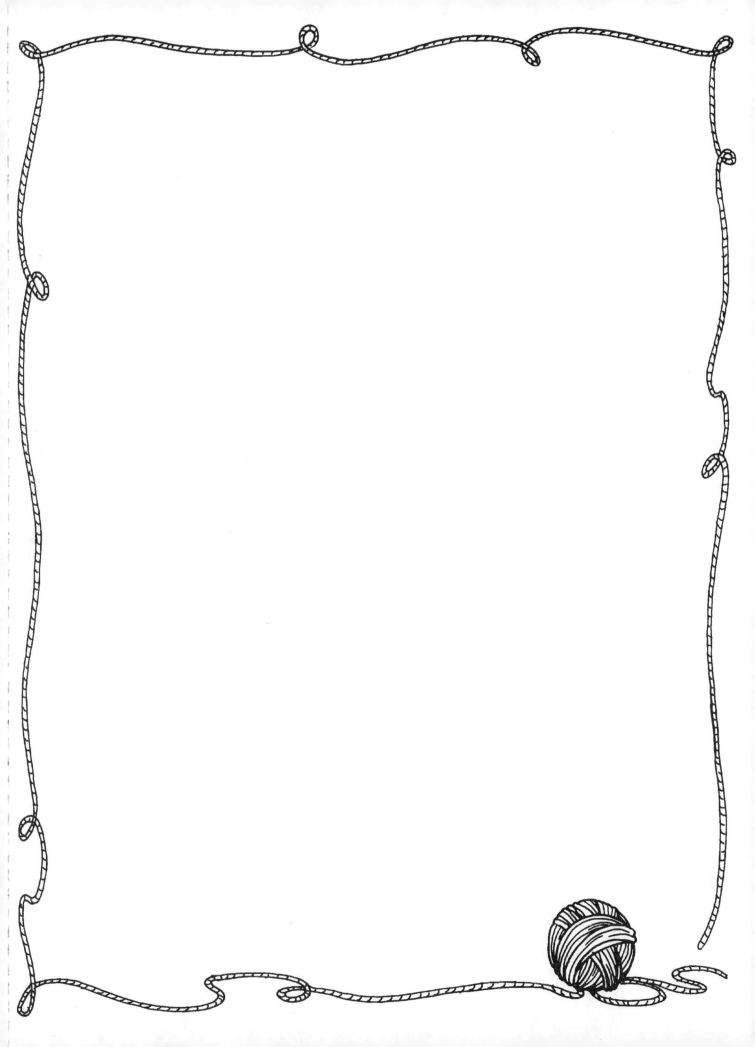

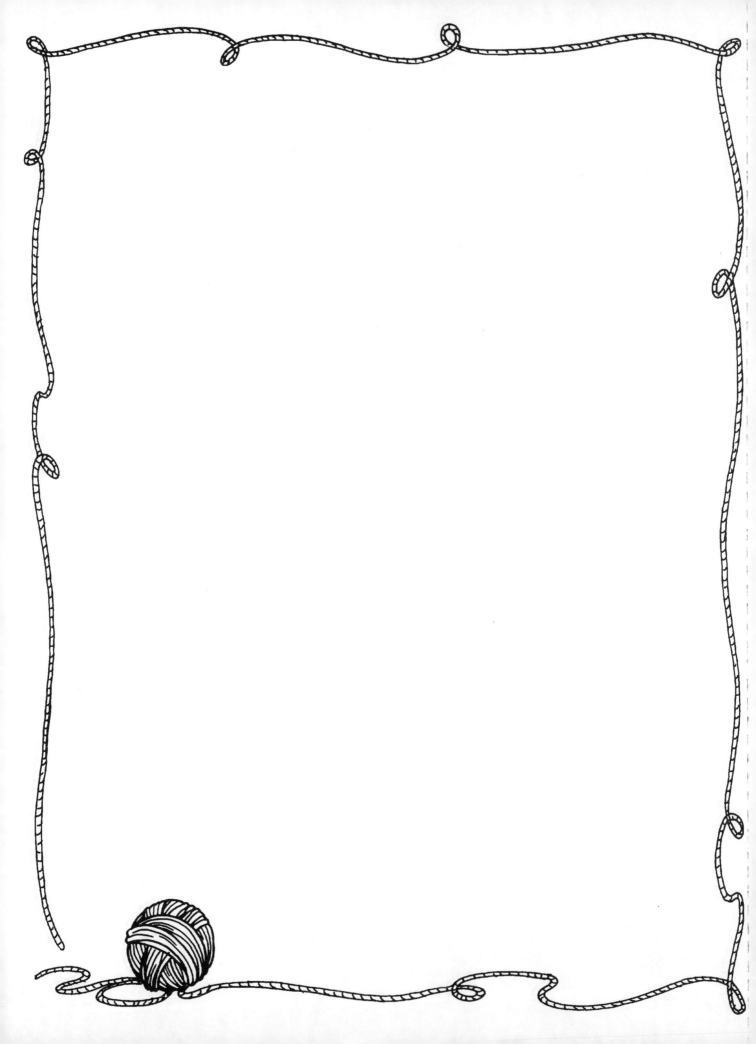

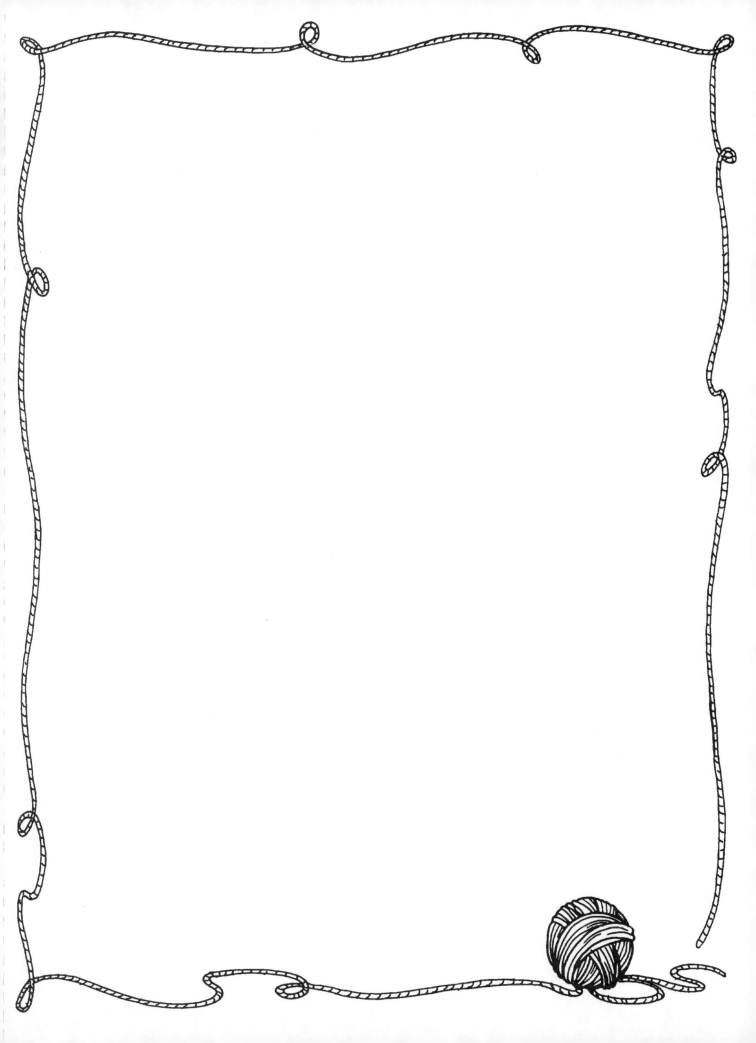

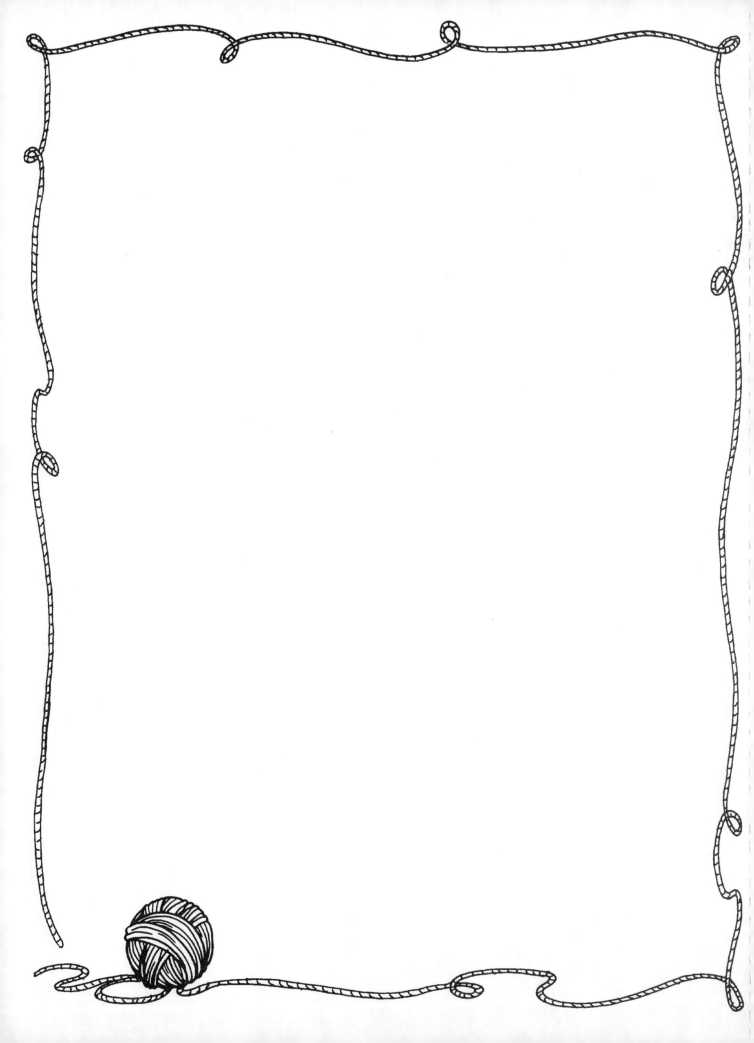

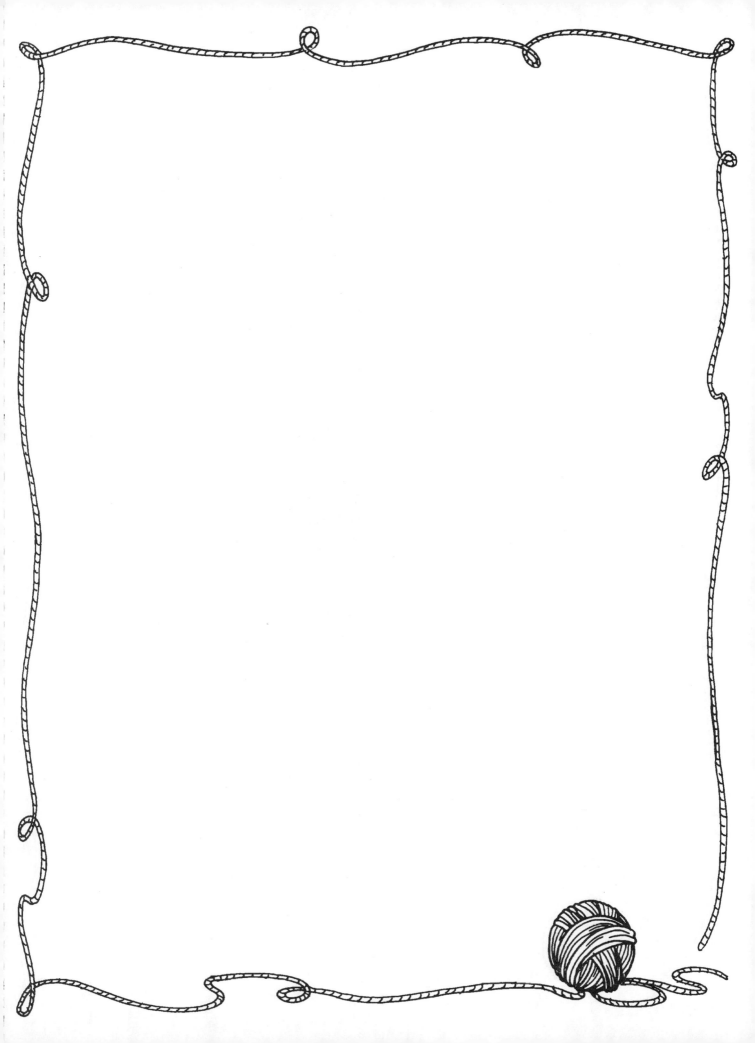

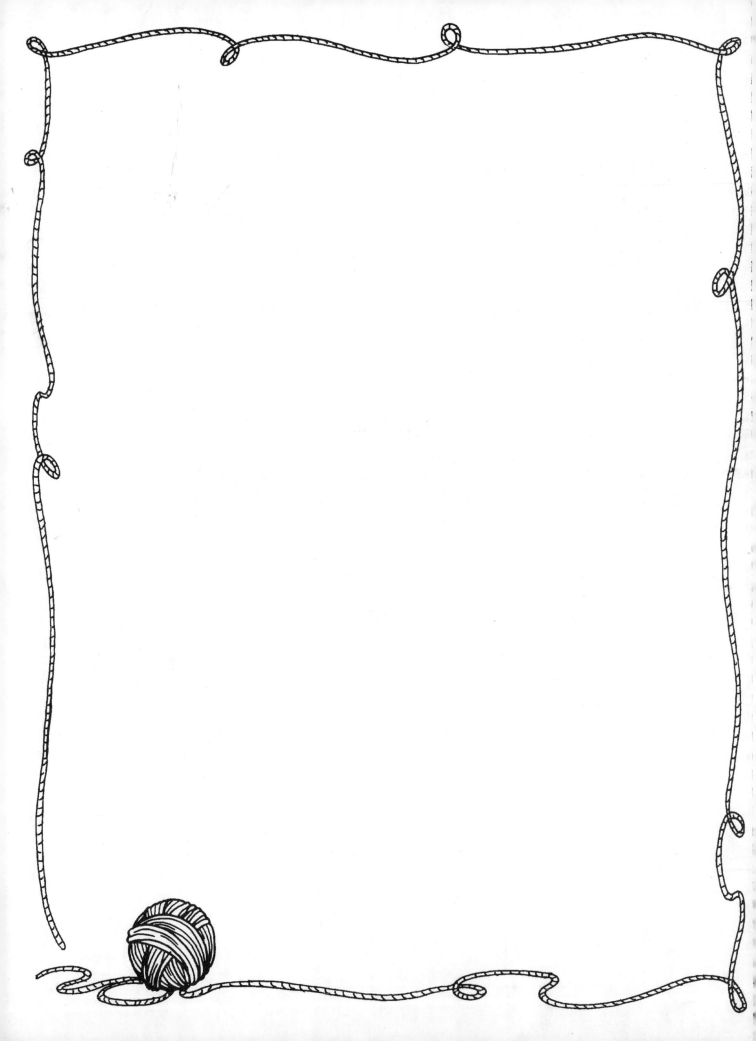